I0842660

THE
SELF-AWAKENING
THROUGH THE
PLANTS & FORESTS

Unleash A Mindful Connection With Nature, Ignite

Consciousness, Cultivate Resilience, and Harmonize Your Life

With the Healing Energy of Plants

by

Dr. MANOJ SARKAR

Dr. ARUNA BASU

Email: manojkumarsarkar1954@gmail.com

Author website: https://niveditatrichy.org

Copyright © 2024 by Manoj Sarkar

All rights reserved. No part of this book may be reproduced in any form without permission in writing from the author.

No part of this publication may be reproduced or transmitted in any form or by any means, mechanical or electronic, including photocopying or recording, by any information storage and retrieval system, or by email or any other means whatsoever without permission in writing from the author.

DEDICATED

TO

OUR REVERED PARENTS

ACKNOWLEDGEMENTS

My humble gratitude to **Mr. Som Bathla**, who is an Amazon #1 **Bestselling author** of multiple books; for mentoring, motivating, and guiding me to **Write, Self-Publish, & Launch Books** and for helping me start my Authorpreneur Journey.

I am thankful to Mr. Ravi Tewari and Mr. Sooraj Achar who is also Amazon #1 **Bestselling authors** of multiple books for their help in publishing this book.

What we are doing to the forests of the world is but a mirror reflection of what we are doing to ourselves and to one another.

- Mahatma Gandhi

The kingdom of plants or kingdom Plantae provides us with 98% of the oxygen we inhale and 80% of the food we eat. The extraordinary kingdom of plants is now under siege. The State of the World's Plants and Fungi Report finds that 40 % of these species face different degrees of threats including even their extinction.

- Craig Brodersen, Times Evoke; TOI, Chennai June 24,2023

Why worry if tigers and rhinos and few plant species are wiped out? An environment in which animals and plants become extinct is not safe for human beings either.

- Indira Gandhi

The Forest is a peculiar organism of unlimited kindness and benevolence that makes no demands for its sustenance and extends the products of its life and activity generously; it affords protection to all beings.

- Buddhist Sutra

TABLE OF CONTENTS

INTRODUCTION

et us start this Introduction with a poem written by **Michael Tierra** about the unleashed wisdom and auspicious healing energy being rendered since time immemorial by the Plant Community to all living beings including mankind:

To all green, growing, flowering ones of this beautiful planet,

who embody the universal creative healing energy,

and with each moment,

humbly assume the ground task of transforming light into life,

and who patiently bear the crude assaults and inserts of our misguided ignorance,

all in the dream of awakening,

Without their conscious, living presence,

Nothing, no breath no food,

no life,

no delight,

None of our earthly endeavors would be possible

"We salute this selfless living Kingdom of Plants with all our humility & take these endeavors in conserving, protecting & propagating them to receive their unleashed wisdom and auspicious healing energy for all."

i) Unleash a mindful connection with nature, ignite consciousness, cultivate resilience, and harmonize your life with the healing energy of plants:

Man is mortal with an average life expectancy of 60 to 80 years. Of course, it varies from developed to developing countries. Within these long years of survival, one may consume 80% of the food products from the plants and 98% of the oxygen also from the plants. The value of this contribution by the plants we understood during the **Pandemic Corona happened** from 2018- 19 onwards. We could observe the fight between man to man for an oxygen cylinder all over the world during this period of crisis, but never give any of our mindful attention to this benevolence Kingdom of plants which provides us the ever.

It may not be with the intention but certainly a lack of awareness of this creature that provides almost everything for us from morning to evening. So, our forgetful nature within needs to be connected with the nature outside. That constitutes both the material and the living entities.

Physical nature constitutes the land mountains, rivers, water, soil, etcetera. Without this platform of physical nature, the biological nature cannot be sustained. So, the external material nature and the living entities of the planet need to have a balanced relationship in healthy and living conditions. When this balanced energy continues, the external and internal nature of the human being merge, that enters in the spiritual world, that is a merging of *Prakriti* and *Purusha* i.e. Matter and Spirit. That is where one is the powerhouse of strength but a blind one (Prakriti- the source of strength)- has no idea where to go, how to go, and how to come out from the jungle of life. While the Purusha- the consciousness of wisdom but a lame person cannot work, cannot walk. So, while they understood each other, the blind strength, the Shakti took the help of a lame-conscious person on her shoulder and the Purusha gave the directions on how to go and come out from the forests.

With cooperation both the Purusha and Prakriti could come out from the jungle. Allegorically, this can be followed by how a human being can remove all jungles of life by connecting his outer nature to the innermost space and coming out for liberation.

ii). Photosynthesis by plants, the release of Oxygen, and their contribution to Human beings and other living entities:

Igniting self-consciousness through the plants and forests is essential for every human being as his or her sustenance for every minute is dependent on the release of oxygen from the plants from the land or the sea. Without food and water, we can survive for a few days but in the absence of Oxygen can we prolong even for a minute! The oxygen released in the atmosphere happens by photosynthesis through a systematic process as narrated below:

A fascinating evolution is the stomata on the underside of leaves of plants. These are microscopic valves that open and close in response to environmental conditions like light, humidity, etc., allowing carbon dioxide to flow into leaves, so the plant can do photosynthesis. Now, when the plant opens these tiny valves, it also exposes the inside of the leaves to the dry atmosphere.

During photosynthesis, plants use sunlight to convert carbon dioxide and water into carbohydrates and oxygen. They take up the carbon dioxide from the ambient air through stomata on the surface of their leaves. At very warm temperatures, however, these close to prevent excessive water loss.

iii). Photosynthesis and the basic products:

As has been stated, carbohydrates are the most important direct organic product of photosynthesis in the majority of green plants. The formation of a simple carbohydrate, glucose, is indicated by a chemical equation.

Formation of a simple carbohydrate, glucose. basic products of photosynthesis:

$$6CO_2 + 12H_2O \xrightarrow[\text{green plants}]{\text{light}} C_6H_{12}O_6 + 6O_2 + 6H_2O.$$

carbon dioxide   water   glucose   oxygen   water

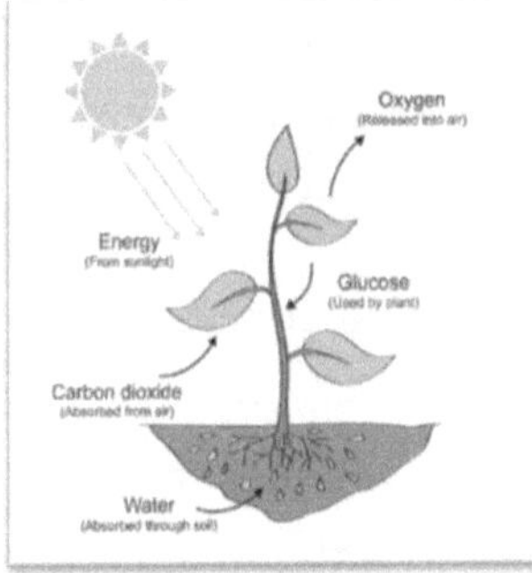

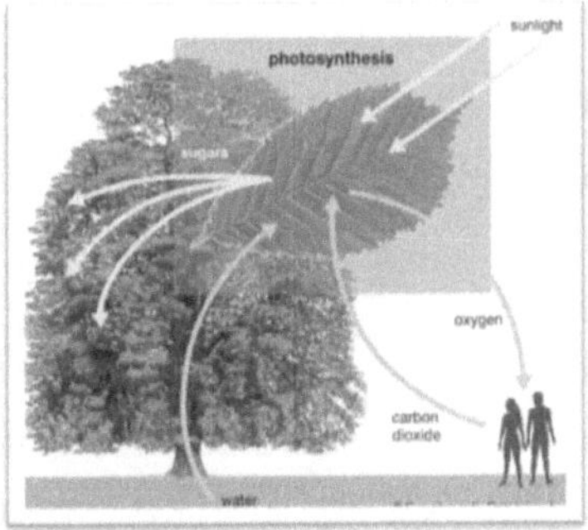

Little free glucose is produced in plants; instead, glucose units are linked to form starch or are joined with fructose, another sugar, to form sucrose.

Not only carbohydrates, as was once thought, but also amino acids, proteins, lipids (or fats), pigments, and other organic components of green tissues are synthesized during photosynthesis. Minerals supply the elements (e.g., nitrogen, N; phosphorus, P; sulfur, S) required to form these compounds.

Chemical bonds are broken between oxygen (O) and carbon (C), hydrogen (H), nitrogen, and sulfur, and new bonds are formed in products that include gaseous oxygen (O2) and organic compounds. More energy is required to break the bonds between oxygen and other elements (e.g., in water, nitrate, and sulfate) than is released when new bonds form in the products. This difference in bond energy accounts for a large part of the light energy stored as chemical energy in the organic products formed during photosynthesis. Additional energy is stored in making complex molecules from simple ones.

Stomata themselves are multiple-consider a banyan tree. This might have 3,50,000 to 5,00,000 stomata on a single leaf. Multiply that by the thousands of leaves on the tree and

Hundreds of millions of these tiny structures open every morning and close by the afternoon, so the plant can conserve water. Millions and millions of stomata on each tree do this daily in response to light intensity and water availability.

When water is limited, the plant closes its stomata, cutting off the CO_2 it normally takes up from the atmosphere. This is because plants figured out the exchange rate relationship very early on - they understood they needed to transport a lot of water, with 95% of this going out into the atmosphere, leaving just 5% to grow plant cells, do a respiration, etc. Having learned this, plants have been fine-tuning their hydraulic pathway or the cells that control water flow in them over millennia.

iv). Importance of photosynthesis:

Photosynthesis is critical for the existence of the vast majority of life on Earth. It is how virtually all energy in the biosphere becomes available to living things. As primary producers, photosynthetic organisms form the base of Earth's food webs and are consumed directly or indirectly by all higher life forms. Additionally, almost all the oxygen in the atmosphere is due to the process of photosynthesis. If photosynthesis ceased, there would soon be little food or other organic matter on Earth, most organisms would disappear, and Earth's atmosphere would eventually become nearly devoid of gaseous oxygen.

Hence, the Self-Awakening about the great contributions being made by the plants to us is the need of the hour for every individual and all of us to work together to protect and augment the plant community.

v). The Plants and Forests:

The **Kingdom of Plants** includes all flora, from minuscule mosses to massive trees on the terrestrial land and the microscopic phytoplankton of various types to the seagrasses in the sea.

Trees, shrubs, herbs, grasses, liana, climbers, stragglers, orchids, etc form the plants from the terrestrial land mass in Forests. While marine plants and plant-like organisms like Phytoplankton live in water. Phytoplankton is microscopic photosynthesizing organisms that include cyanobacteria, green algae, diatoms, dinoflagellates, etc. Although too small to be visible to the human eye by itself, when many phytoplankton clump together they look like green ocean slime.

Both the plants from the land and the sea together produce 98% of the oxygen we inhale and 80% of the food we eat. According to National Geographic, about 70% of the oxygen in the atmosphere comes from marine plants and plant-like organisms.

vi). Forests - the home of the Plants works as the Basic Life Supporting System (BLISS!) for all living beings including mankind:

The Kingdom of Plants or the Kingdom of Plantae is the only living entity that sacrifices everything for the benefit of all living beings including mankind. The forests in the Sea and on landmass - the home of the Plant kingdom work as a storehouse to supply all the Basic Life Supporting Systems (BLISS!). Besides tangible and intangible benefits flow, the Kingdom of Plants also extends subtle blessings and wisdom to the aspirants through their spirit of unending services in silence as Monks who care for them. Thus, forests as a composition of innumerable plants on land and sea operate as the 'Sea of Monks' being the panacea for human beings and other living organisms. These very facts urge for a committed, logical, and scientific approach to protect, conserve, manage, and expand our forest resources for the present as well as for the generations to come.

A forest is an ecosystem dominated by trees. According to the parameters established by the FAO, an area must cover at least half a hectare, or about one and a quarter acre, to be considered a forest. The trees in the area must also be able to grow to heights above 16 feet and have a canopy that covers at least 10% of the sky.

(Despite the precise definition laid out by the FAO, there is still controversy over what constitutes a forest because the current forest definition does not distinguish between forest types, it can be difficult to monitor changes in the amount of forest.)

We acknowledge the source of everything that is in this book and accept our indebtedness to that infinite source of strength that exists in all living beings, especially in the form of the kingdom of plants, which pulled us affectionately and instilled all wisdom documented in this book through their selfless service in silence.

PART I: AWARENESS CREATION FOR PLANTS, AND FORESTS

1. Global Forest Types, Plant Compositions, and Their Location

The world's forests are diverse and can be broadly categorized into several major types based on their characteristics, geographical locations, and the predominant plant species they contain. The main types of forests found around the world are narrated below based on their floral compositions, biodiversity, and also the major causes of deforestation:

1. Tropical Rainforests:

Located around the equator in regions such as the Amazon Basin, Congo Basin, and Southeast Asia. High temperatures, high humidity, and consistent rainfall resulted in extremely diverse flora and fauna.

Characterized by a dense and diverse array of plant life, including towering trees like mahogany, teak, and ebony. Epiphytes, such as orchids and bromeliads, are common, and the understory is filled with ferns and various shrubs. Home to a vast array of plant and animal species, including many endemic and endangered species

Logging, Agriculture Infrastructure Development, and Mining are the Major Causes of deforestation Characterized by a dense and diverse array of plant life, including towering trees like mahogany, teak, and ebony. Epiphytes, such as orchids and bromeliads, are common, and the understory is filled with ferns and various shrubs. Home to a vast array of plant and animal species, including many endemic and endangered species. Logging, Agriculture Infrastructure Development, and Mining are the Major Causes of deforestation

2. Temperate Forests:

Found in temperate regions, including parts of North America, Europe, and East Asia. Moderate temperatures with distinct seasons. Deciduous trees that shed leaves in the fall. Eastern Deciduous Forest in North America, European Temperate Forests, and East Asian Forests.

Dominated by deciduous trees that shed their leaves in the fall, including oak, maple, beech, and hickory. The understory often includes flowering plants, ferns, and mosses. Rich in bird species, mammals like deer and bears, etc.

3. Boreal Forests (Taiga):

Located in High latitudes, mostly in the Northern Hemisphere. Northern regions of North America, Europe, and Asia. Cold temperatures, coniferous trees (evergreen needle-leaved), and a relatively short growing season. Siberian Taiga, Canadian Boreal Forest, Scandinavian Taiga. Predominantly composed of coniferous trees like spruce, fir, and pine. Ground vegetation includes mosses, lichens, and hardy shrubs adapted to cold climates. It is inhabited by species such as moose, wolves, and migratory birds.

4. Temperate Rainforests:

Found along the western coasts of North America, including the Pacific Northwest, and parts of New Zealand and

Chile. Mild temperatures, high rainfall, and evergreen trees. More temperate than tropical rainforests.

Characterized by dense vegetation of evergreen trees such as redwoods and Douglas firs. Mosses, ferns, and other understorey vegetation thrive in the moist environment. Diverse wild fauna such as bears, cougars, and various bird species are found here

5. Mediterranean Forests:

Located around the Mediterranean Sea and other regions with a Mediterranean climate. Mediterranean Basin, California Chaparral, South African Fynbos. Hot, dry summers and mild, wet winters. Dominated by evergreen trees and shrubs.

6. Montane Forests:

Located in Mountainous regions at various latitudes. Varied based on altitude, with temperature and vegetation changing with elevation. Montane Rainforests in the Andes, Rocky Mountains, and Himalayan Montane Forests.

Floral Composition varies with altitude but may include a mix of coniferous and broadleaf trees. Alpine plants adapted to harsh conditions, such as lichens and dwarf shrubs, become prevalent at higher elevations.

Species in these forests have adapted to the challenging conditions of high altitudes, and they often include unique plant and animal species not found in lower elevations.

7. Dry Forests:

Situated in Arid and semi-arid regions. Found in regions with a pronounced dry season, such as parts of Africa, Asia, and the Americas. Thorn Forests in Africa, Dry Forests in Australia. Typically consists of drought-resistant trees and shrubs, such as acacias, baobabs, and succulent plants. Many species shed leaves during the dry season to conserve water. Animals like camels, kangaroos, and various reptiles are from here

8. Polar Ice Cap and Tundra:

Located around the polar regions, with Cold temperatures, permafrost, and low-lying vegetation. Arctic Tundra, Antarctic Tundra.

These forest types are critical for global biodiversity, climate regulation, and the well-being of ecosystems. They face various threats, including deforestation, climate change, and habitat destruction, emphasizing the importance of conservation efforts.

2. Share in the Percentage of Global Forest Area, 2020 of Various Countries

(Source: UN Food and Agriculture Organisation (FAO) Forest Resources Assessment.)

The major share of global forest area, in 2020 is as follows:

The European countries have a maximum of 25.07% mainly with Temperate types of forests with coniferous trees as they are located in mid-latitudes to towards polar region.

South America possesses 20.8% forest cover mainly with Tropical Rain Forests full of biodiversity and high-density valuable forests covering mainly Brazil, Bolivia, and Peru as they are near the equatorial regions.

Africa is almost without much forest cover except for the Democratic Republic of Congo, Angola, Zambia, and Tanzania have Tropical rainforests because of their nearness to the equatorial zone and cover 15.68% of forests.

Asian countries have tropical, sub-tropical, and Mangrove Forest cover of 15.34% with China, and India being the main countries. The rest covers Oceania with only 4.56 % of forest.

Figure -1 Shows the Share of the global forest area, in 2020 on the map below:

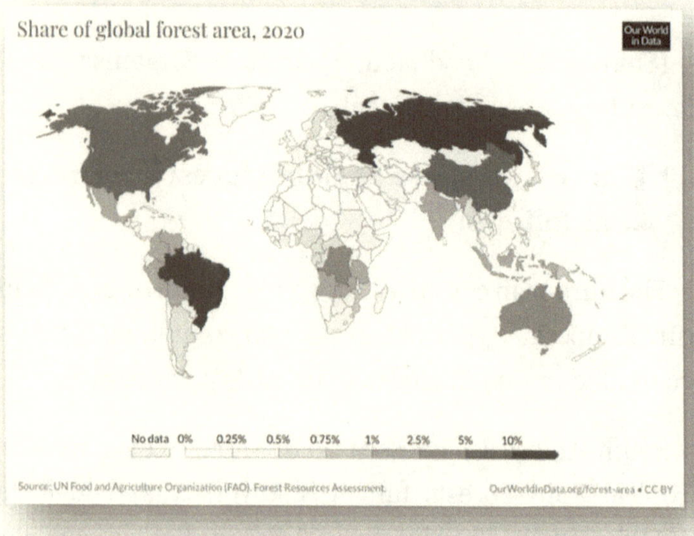

3. Global threat Status of Plants and Forests

i) Threat Status of Plants:

The species extinction rate has increased many-fold over the years due to the ever-increasing human population and anthropogenic activities, bringing to the forefront the 'sixth mass extinction' crisis (Shivanna 2020).

The estimated number of threatened species in Kingdom Plantae, Animalia, Chromista, and Fungi, globally and in India as per the IUCN assessment (IUCN 2020) is clearly shown in Figure -2.

Total number of threatened species of Kingdom Plantae, Animalia, Chromista, and Fungi at global and Indian national level as per IUCN estimation.

The numerical values mentioned on the arrows indicate the number of threatened species (Source: IUCN 2020). More than 50% of the world's plant species are endemic to 35 Global Biodiversity Hotspots (GBH).

These hotspots shelter a large number of endemic species, which are facing an increasing threat of extinction (Hazarika et al. 2016).

Figure. 2-Total number of threatened species of Kingdom Plantae, Animalia, Chromista, and Fungi at global and Indian national level as per IUCN estimation.

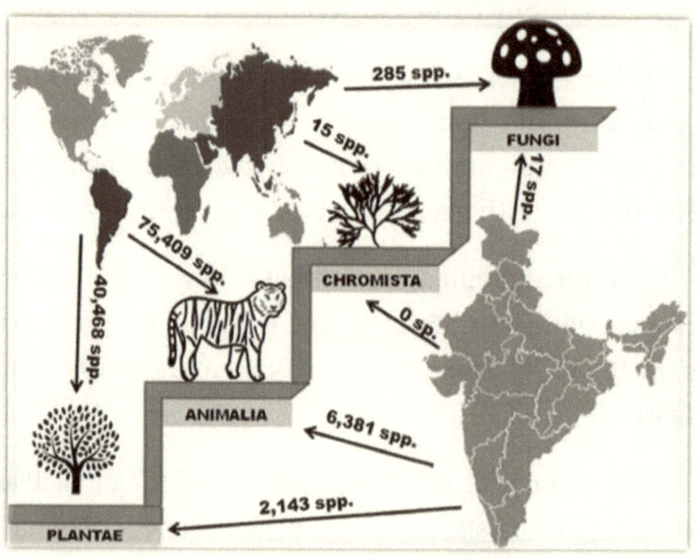

(Source: IUCN 2020)

On a global basis, IUCN has estimated that about 13.49% of the world's vascular plants (3,00,000 species), totaling about 40,468 species are under varying degrees of threat.

Break-up details are shown in Table -1. It is estimated that India has 10.45% of global floral diversity. In India, about 11.53% of vascular plants (18,532), totaling about 2,142 species are red-listed.

Details are given in Table -2 below.

Table – 1 Numbers of Families, Genera, and Globally Threatened Vascular Plants

	World Total	Extinct		Threatened plant species			Lower Risk plant species			
		EX	EW	CR	EN	VU	LR /cd	NT	LC	DD
Total Species Count	3,00,000	EX	EW	CR	EN	VU	LR /cd	NT	LC	DD
No, of Threatened Plant species	40,468	123	37	3325	6063	7072	171	2500	18403	2774

Table – 2 Status of Threatened Vascular Plants in India

	India Total	Extinct		Threatened plant species			Lower Risk plant species			
		EX	EW	CR	EN	VU	LR/cd	NT	LC	DD
Total Species Count	18,532	EX	EW	CR	EN	VU	LR/cd	NT	LC	DD
No, of Threatened Plant species	2143	6	2	86	191	155	1	54	1545	103

Table 1. and 2: Number of plant species threatened at the Global and National level as per IUCN estimation (EX: Extinct; EW- Extinct in the Wild; CR-Critically Endangered; EN: Endangered; VU: Vulnerable; LR/cd: Lower Risk-Conservation Dependent; NT: Near threatened; LC: Least concern; DD; Data deficient (Source: IUCN 2020)

ii)   Global threat Status of Forests:

In 2009, two-thirds of the world's forests were located in just 10 countries: Russia, Brazil, Canada, the United States, China, Australia, the Democratic Republic of the Congo, Indonesia, India, and Peru.

Rates and causes of deforestation vary from region to region around the world. In decades since 1990, South America and Africa have shown the greatest loss of forest area, with global net loss in the 2010s still about 60% of the 1990s value.

Global annual deforestation is estimated to total 13.7 million hectares a year, equal to the area of Greece. Half of the area experiencing deforestation consists of new forests or forest growth. In addition to direct human-induced deforestation, growing forests have also been affected by climate change. The Kyoto Protocol includes an agreement to prevent deforestation but does not stipulate actions to fulfill it.

The list of countries and territories of the world according to the total area covered by forests, is based on data published by the **Food and Agriculture Organization of the United Nations (FAO).** In 2010, the world had 3.92 billion hectares (ha) of tree cover, extending over 30% of its land area. In 2022, it lost 22.8 million ha of tree cover

In 2020, the world had a total forest area of 4.06 billion ha, which was 31 percent of the total land area. This area is equivalent to 0.52 ha per person – although forests are not distributed equally among the world's people or geographically. The tropical domain has the largest proportion of the world's forests (45 percent), followed by the boreal, temperate, and subtropical domains. More than half (54 percent) of the world's forests are in only five countries – the Russian Federation (20.1%), Brazil (12.2%), Canada (8.6%), the United States of America (7.6%), and China (5.4%).

Many of the world's forests are being damaged and degraded or are disappearing altogether. Their capacity to provide tangible goods, such as fiber, food, and medicines, as well as essential ecological services, including habitat for biodiversity, carbon storage, and moderation of freshwater flows, is under greater threat than ever before. According to World Resource Institute in Washington, between 2000 and 2020 the world lost 101 million hectares (Mha) of tree cover, mostly tropical and subtropical forests (92%). The FAO is compiling a new global assessment due to be published in 2025.

Net Change in Global Forest Area

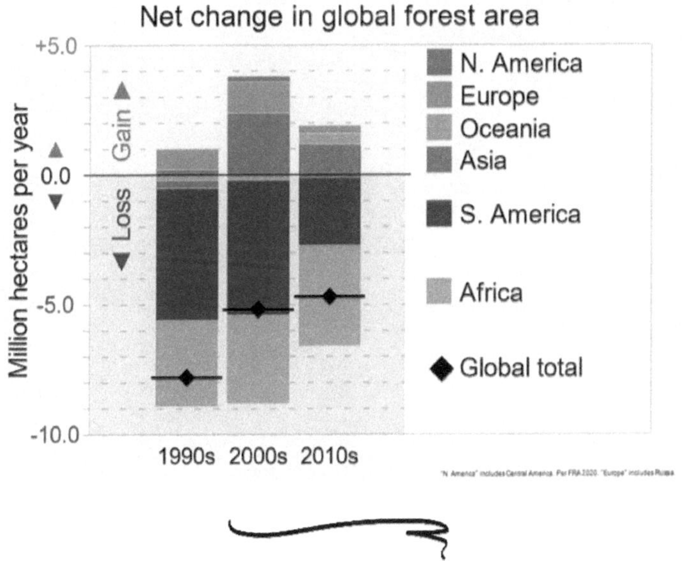

4. The Art of living in Symbiotic Relationship with Flora, Fauna, and Man

Living- long with all our surrounding natural ecosystems in our locality, in our country then with the globe is far better and healthier than living alone within the boundary of the wall of our own. On the same line Revd. Rabindranath Tagore- the famous Noble laurite mentioned this in a poem from his book GITANJALI- The Offerings of Songs as quoted below.

"Where the mind is without fear and the head is held high;

Where knowledge is free;

Where the world has not broken up into fragments of narrow domestic walls;

Where words come out from the depth of truth;

Where tireless striving stresses its arms toward perfection;

Where the clear stream of reason has not lost its way into the dreary desert sand of dead habit;

Where the mind is laid forward by thee into ever-widening thought and action—

Into that heaven of freedom, my father let my country awake."

Truly speaking, none of us is alone in our journey of life. We all are connected. Our time of arrival and the time of departure may vary but the state of performance remains where all living beings, the flora covering from minuscule mosses to massive trees on land, then phytoplankton, sea grasses, etc in the sea continue to play their role as service to all living entities including the mankind.

The micro creatures, the ants, earthworms, and many other faunae help us to grow fertile soil to provide us with food, while butterflies and other insects help in pollination.

Similarly, the fauna from the micro creatures to ants to butterflies to elephants to whales, all continue their duty with a symbiotic relationship. But we, human beings get all the facilities free of cost without even thinking about how we inhale every moment and survive. It is all from the providence of the community of plants on the mother earth.

At the time of pandemic corona, we understood the value of oxygen and its cost and crisis for O2 cylinders! Even then, we remain immune to the fact of this and continue to fight each other with modern lethal weapons putting the entire glove under threat. In the name of so-called development every day we cut the trees, and deforest the virgin forests at the cost of ourselves and also for the progeny to come! The ultimate result is climate change with Cloud bursts, frequent floods, Drought un common snowfall, sea levels, etc.

So, the time has come to arise, awake, and stop not till our goal is achieved to put our selfless service to stop deforestation and take active care for the plants and forests to grow, protect, and conserve them to flourish for the prolonged benefit of all living beings.

As research in the Proceedings of the National Academy of Sciences USA finds, with over 4.00,000 known species, they account for 80% of the total biomass or life forms on Earth. Bacteria come second at a distant 15% - humans are 0.01%

There are living trees, and their ages are more than 1000 to 10,000 years or even more, they continue to serve us along with other smaller plants including small trees, shrubs, herbs, climbers, liana even grasses serve us with O2 and absorb CO2 from the atmosphere. The old leaves and fallen dead branches continue to add humus, colloids, and micronutrients to the soil. There are even smaller plants who take care to bless us. They communicate intuitively to the individuals to provide the solution to man's problems.

5. Forest Bathing or Shinrin yoku as practiced by the Japanese

The Japanese practice of shinrin yoku, or Forest Bathing, is good for both physical and mental well-being. It is proven to reduce stress hormone production, improve feelings of happiness, and free up creativity, as well as lower heart rate and blood pressure, boost the immune system, and accelerate recovery from illness.

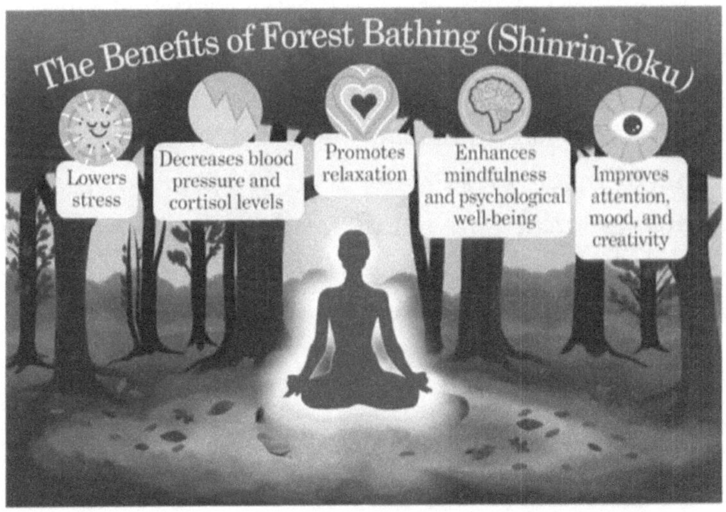

The benefits of Forest Bathing

Forest Bathing is a powerful antidote to the pressures of the modern world, proven to deliver lasting benefits to your physical and mental wellbeing, and creating within you a profound connection to nature. On a Forest Bathing experience, our fully qualified Forest Therapy Guides lead you through a series of activities that use the healing powers of the forest to help you re-balance your mind and body.

Originating in Japan - you may have seen it called shinrin yoku - Forest Bathing is an accepted part of Japanese preventative health care because of the mental, physical, and spiritual health benefits it delivers. Also known as forest therapy, it draws on thousands of years of intuitive knowledge - we are part of nature and we have a deep need to feel that connection.

Forest Bathing has been around as a concept in Japan since the early 1980s and scientists there continue to conduct a large amount of research into its benefits, concluding that it deserves its place in the Japanese healthcare system. *More general research into the area of nature connections suggests that the real and long-term benefits include, among other things, reduced stress, improved immunity, lower blood pressure, and accelerated recovery from illness or trauma.*

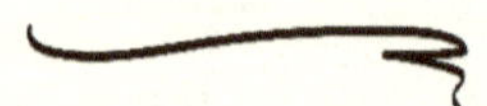

PART II: LEARN TO LOVE THE PLANTS, PROTECT, CONSERVE, AND AUGMENT THEM FROM FELLINGS; THAT NEEDS SACRIFICE LIKE PLANTS

Chipko Movement- "Huge the Trees" - not allow them to cut. Revered personalities like Sundar Lal Bahuguna, Chandi Prasad Bhat started the movement from the Himalayas during ... needs to be continued all over the glove to save the Earth.

6. True Love Never Expects Anything in Return

True love never expects anything in return. Before our birth, the Kingdom of Plants kept ready our Roti, Kapra, and Mokan which is our food to eat, oxygen to inhale to connect our Prana-- the vital energy of our body to the universe and the shelter to protect us from the Sun, Rain and Cold. These are the basic life-supporting systems (Bliss) provided by the kingdom Plantae to all the living beings on this planet.

Plant antiquity far surpasses human beings and all other worlds of fauna. Land plants first appeared 500 million years ago on Earth (humans are just six million years old), with trees emerging 370 million years ago. Crucially, as plants increased, they removed more and more carbon dioxide from the atmosphere. cooling Earth and emitting oxygen, enabling animals. Indeed, it was the majestic science of plants- their photosynthesis turns water, sunlight, and CO, into oxygen and sugars - that made human life possible through the gifts of air and food.

Their beauty can encourage many to think of plants as just Earth's whimsical ornaments - but the fact is, the kingdom Plantae gives humanity 80% of the food we eat and 98% of the oxygen we breathe.

This extraordinary kingdom is now under siege. The State of the World's Plants and Fungi Report finds that 40% of these species face extinction, confronting the large-scale destruction of habitat for commercial farming, livestock rearing, and construction. Plants are also embattled by climate change, caused by anthropogenic emissions altering Earth's air, water, and heat, triggering floods, droughts, fires, and pestilence. The Food and Agriculture Organization (FAO) finds that 40% of all crops are already lost annually, leaving millions facing hunger. But there are solutions too - as Times Evoke's global experts emphasize, plant literacy is key.

It is only by learning of these species', foundational importance that we will preserve them. Human history has witnessed many forms of rule, the longest being regency, which meant copyrighted exploitation, accompanied by fervent slogans to protect a regent, a leader, a human symbol of power. Join Times Evoke in changing this way of thought - and thinking more imaginatively. 'God save the green'. Our lives depend on plants – We must have plant literacy to understand climate change. 1.

We all human beings without expecting name, fame, money, or even the result of our actions, should love this benevolent kingdom of plants by protecting, conserving, and helping them in propagating through our thoughts, words, and actions.

This formula or the life mantra was followed by our Hero Mr. HUGO WOOD (Hugo Francies Andrew Wood, 1870-1933) in 1916-17 to bring back the lost glory of the greeneries of the Anamalai range in Western Ghats, India as explained in my last book (Self- Mastery and Enlightenment through the

Kingdom of Plants, published through Amazon platform, on 26th January 2024). That would be the real love towards the Kingdom of Plants with a positive mindset in serving them to save all living beings including us with our progeny in the years to come.

7. The power of Sacrifice, Charity, and Austerity connect us with the Power of the Universe/Cosmic Unified Force

Selfless activities in Thought, Words, and Action do not bind oneself from the bondage of life. Karma or the activities is inevitable for each individual. Selfless activities without any expectation from the result of karma can help in getting liberated. Amongst all activities, Selfless services like Sacrifice, charity, and Austerity bring us closer to the door of liberation.

"Let such sacrifice be your fulfilling cow of plenty. " This sacrifice will satisfy the Almighty- the source of all energy of the Universe. Almighty in turn will satisfy your needs. This is the mutual arrangement that will get you the greatest good in life.

The Sense is superior to Sense objects, the Mind is superior to the senses, and Superior to the mind is the Intellect. Superior even to the intellect is the Self.

So, to get ever connected with the Self, one has to Sacrifice the best (maybe the Wisdom! to the desirable persons) and be ever connected with the existence consciousness bliss Absolute. The concepts of Sacrifice, Charity, and Austerity are noble activities that are not to be abandoned by us but to be practiced consistently as prescribed in Shrimad Bhagwat Geeta by Lord Srikrishna in the 18th Chapter. It elaborates further as Renunciation means, Giving up the results of the material activity i.e. Tyaga or Sacrifice

Some learned individuals say that certain activities, being inherently faulty, should be abandoned as evil, while others say that sacrifice, benevolence, and austerity should never be relinquished. However, as per the scripture renunciation is of three kinds. These are Sacrifice, Charity, and Austerity.

The acts of sacrifice, charity, and austerity are not to be given up, rather these should be performed, as the acts of sacrifice, charity, and austerity purify even the wise persons. However, these actions need to be performed without any attachment or expectation of results. These should be performed as a duty.

These have deep roots in various religious, spiritual, and philosophical traditions. The deeper perspectives suggest that engaging in these practices can connect individuals with a higher or cosmic force, often referred to as the Universe, Cosmic Unified Force, or a similar concept. Let's explore each of these concepts and realize how these are already being by the plant community millions of years before arrival of the human beings

Like the plants, as they provide us the Basic life supporting system for our food, o2, and shelter through their noble act of sacrifice, we must reciprocate similar activities to protect them to protect ourselves. The act of sacrifice like plants will align oneself with a greater cosmic order. By willingly letting go of certain attachments or comforts, we may attune ourselves to the energy or consciousness that permeates the universe.

Acts of charity are thought to foster a sense of interconnectedness with the larger goals. By extending help to others, individuals express recognition of the inherent unity that binds all living beings as the services already being rendered by the kingdom of plants to all of us. Likewise, we must appreciate and realize the benevolence characteristics of the plant community and extend our support with mindfulness

Austerity purifies the mind and body, stripping away distractions and attachments. This purification process is thought to open channels for individuals to connect with the cosmic force or universal energy that underlies all existence.

In summary, the common thread among sacrifice, charity, and austerity is the belief that these practices help individuals transcend the personal ego and align with a larger, cosmic order. By letting go of individual desires, reaching out to others in need, and practicing self-discipline, individuals may seek to tap into the profound and interconnected energy that some perceive as the Cosmic Unified Force.

PART III: VOLITION IN SERVING PEOPLE BY CREATING AWARENESS ABOUT THE GOODNESS OF PLANTS THROUGH DAILY NEWSPAPERS

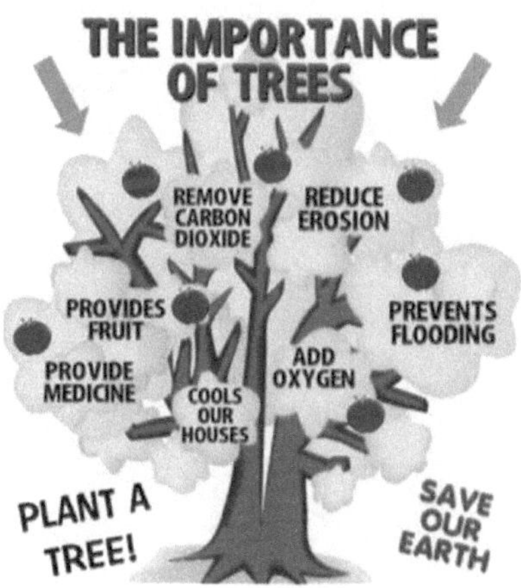

The following articles were retyped and placed herein for the convenience of the learned readers as follows:

a. Develop and implement educational programs that emphasize the importance of plants in our lives.

b. Encourage people to participate in activities that involve plants, such as gardening, and to learn more about them.

c. Support initiatives that promote the protection and conservation of plants, such as planting native species and advocating for policy change.

d. Create public awareness campaigns that highlight the value of plants and how they contribute to our lives.

e. Establish incentives and rewards for people who take steps to protect plants.

f. Make sure that plants are included in the curriculum of schools and other educational.

8. AGAVE, a Multipurpose Dryland Plant

(Published in "The Hindu . on the Science and Technology Page")

Agave in the nursery- ready for planting for soil binding and fibers for livelihood

AGAVE is a large genus of short-stemmed half-woody plants bearing a rosette of long, erect, pointed, fleshy leaves. About 275 species of the Agavaceae family are distributed in tropical South America. Six species of *Agave anguistifolia, A. americana. A. hurida A. camtala, A. sisalana,* and *A. vera-cruz* were introduced in India during the 15th century by the Portuguese. These are now completely naturalized and cultivated in different parts of the country, particularly in the dry zones. In South India, they are called Kathaalai (in Tamil), Kithanara, Kalpataru (in Telugu), and Rakas patta (in Hindi).

Cultivation of four varieties of *Agave americana, A. cantala, A. sisalana,* and *A. vera cruz* has proved beneficial. The plant has locally been used as a medicine for a long time. Generally, it is grown as a live fence. Its widespread root system serves as a good soil binder and so it is also used to check soil erosion by planting across gullies and slopes. Farmers in the arid and semiarid regions of South India comprising Tamil Nadu, Karnataka Andhra Pradesh, Maharashtra, and Orrisa grow it for its medicinal properties and for its fiber (used in making ropes).

Farmers in the arid and semi-arid regions of south India comprising Tamil Nadu, Karnataka, Andhra Pradesh, Maharashtra, and Orissa grow it for its medicinal properties and for its fiber (used in making ropes)

Their leaves contain an alkaloid called hecogenin. Its juice is considered to be a laxative, diuretic, and emmenagogue. It is also used as a resolvent in syphilis, scrofula, and cancer.

Thin slices of the leaves are used as a good poultice. The leaves are heated, split, and applied to painful spots in rheumatic patients to relieve pain. The plants can grow in poor, infertile soil and rocky terrains.

Agave americana or American aloe has large silvery-grey leaves. They are thick, fleshy, and covered with a thick cuticle and a coating of wax. The margins of the leaf are pricky and the leaf itself ends in a spiny pointed tip. After a long growth period, say 60 years (sometimes 100 years) the plant produces flowers and a huge inflorescence held aloft a huge and robust flesh stalk.

A native of Mexico and Central America plants find a natural home in the dry and hot regions of the Deccan peninsula. The young flower head on cutting yields a large quantity of juice which on fermentation yields pulque, the national drink of Mexico. The distilled liquor (alcohol content of 3-4 percent) is known as mescal. The plant is used as a fish poison, and the plant's core is used as a febrifuge in malaria. It is used as an antiseptic and also in ascites, venereal sores, and dysentery.

A. cantala a perennial stout scapigerous plant with a short woody stem, is native to Mexico. Its leaves appear in rosettes forming a crown, which is recurved on the upper surface. It is remotely spinescently dentate with 1-2 cm long upwardly hooked spines and scaly stout scapes. It is grown as a hedge and thrives well on fairly good soil and in regions with rainfall of 100-250 cm. The leaves yield a fiber of 3-4.5 percent of their weight, which is roughly about 6.4 tonnes/ha.

A. sisalana is a perennial short-stemmed herb, that is cultivated in many parts of India. Its stem, 37.5 cm thick, bears a dark green rosette. It has thick, fleshy, rigid 10-15 cm long leaves which are 10-15 cm wide at the broadest portion. It is generally without spines on the margins with yellow flowers.

A. vera-cruz, a stout perennial herb 30-45 cm tall, with a woody simple stem has long, erect spinescently dentate leaves. It has flowers in terminal panicles.

The stem contains polyfructosans besides several simple sugars as minor constituents. The soft woody portion of the stem is cooked with tamarind and jaggery in some parts of South India. While small quantities of the stem may be safely consumed, ingestion of large amounts produces gastrointestinal disorders. The leaves yield a fiber (cellulose 75 percent, lignin 15 percent) which is coarser and stronger than cantala fibre and is used in making ropes, cordage, and mats.

Agave angustifolia the dwarf Aloe, Seemakathaalai (in Tamil), Kantala (in Sanskrit) and

Balurakkasi (in Telugu), is a perennial herb with a stout trunk, still leaves in a compact rosette, and flowers in terminal panicles. It is used as an ornamental plant and is now naturalized in the outer Himalayas and other parts. It is grown as a hedge in gardens and along railway lines and is very common throughout Purandhar (Maharashtra).

A. hurida is an almost trunkless shrub, with leaves that are 0.9 m long and 15 cm wide. This was also introduced for its fibre which is shorter and somewhat stiffer than the other agave fibres. Mature leaves can be harvested from 3-4-year-old plants and from the fifth year onwards regular harvesting of leaves can be done for extracting fibre.

People in Tiruchy and Dindigul instead of collecting the mature leaves from the lower sides of the plant, collect the central stem axis cone (consisting of 15 to 20 immature leaves) beat them, and extract the fiber. This damages the plant which takes a long time to grow. Such practice has to be discouraged.

Retting and mechanical methods are used for fiber extraction. In the retting process, the leaves after harvesting are immersed in water for about a week. During this period the pithy matter adhering to fibres disintegrates due to bacterial action. The retted leaves are then beaten on stones to remove the remaining extraneous matter. The separated fiber is washed, dried in the sun, and baled. In the mechanical process, the fiber is extracted by rasping the leaves with a raspador. Raspador is a rotating drum mounted on an axle having blunt blades, fitted obliquely about 10 cm apart on its periphery. The leaves are fed into the slit of the raspador and pulled out. By this method, almost the entire extraneous matter is removed leaving only the fibre strand. The fiber is then soaked in water for about 10 minutes to remove the remaining green pigments and beaten on stone, washed again, and dried.

The entire family is engaged in the fiber extraction process and sustains the livelihood

The dried fiber is combed with a special knife to remove the remains of pithy matter; combing also renders the fiber lustrous. In India, both methods of fiber extraction are practiced, though retting is common.

In some states, cooperative societies and private units are engaged in the fiber supply. Some quantity is locally used for the preparation of twines, ordinary ropes, bags, hats, and nets. The sisal waste is used in the manufacture of a hard lustrous wax which is a good substitute for carnauba wax. Experiments carried out at the National Chemical Laboratory, Pune, have indicated that the yield of wax is 8-18 percent of the waste materials depending on the quality of the waste.

In Andhra Pradesh. fiber is extracted using a manually operated device in which the leaves are bruised and the cuticle and internal sap are removed. The fibers are then cleared, dried, and packed. The waste (pulp) obtained after processing is used as a manure. In Maharashtra, cantala fiber is extracted on a commercial scale by the retting process. Mechanically decorticated fiber is finer but less tensile than sisal. The fiber is used for ropes, mats, cordage, twines, and nets. Cantala fiber is pure white, whereas sisal is light yellow.

In India, sisal is cultivated in Andra Pradesh, Assam, West Bengal, Bihar, Orissa, Tamil Nadu, Maharashtra and Karnataka. Sisal grows well on dry, permeable sandy loam soils and is highly drought resistant. It is reported to thrive well in areas with low rainfall. The leaves are cut for fiber between the third and fourth year. The lowest leaves are cut close to the trunk. Each plant yields 250-300 leaves during the 7-8 years of its lifetime.

Farmers in Tiruchy. Dindigul, Salem, and Dharmapuri of Tamil Nadu collect the agave leaves for fiber which are made into ropes and sold. The average annual production of sisal fiber in India is estimated at 12,000 tonnes, whereas the total demand for agave is well over 50,000 tonnes. Annually, India imports agave worth Rs. 2.5 crores from Tanzania, Kenya, and other countries. However, India exports sisal ropes and twines to Nepal and Fiji Islands.

Due to its many favorable characteristics, various government departments have taken up agave planting in field boundaries, reserved forests, and in barren lands. Such planting serves to check soil erosion and provides alternative sources of Income to the local villagers. In Tamil Nadu, the Forest Department has a specific division called Agave Division at Coimbatore.

Rope making from Agave fiber

Agave propagation can be carried out either by bulbils or root suckers. The bulbils are collected between March and May every year (it varies from species to species). The collected bulbils are then planted in primary beds (size 10m x 1m) at an espacement of 5cm × 5cm. Flood watering is done once in three days for six months. Weeding is done twice a month. After six months (that is when the seedlings are 20-30 cm high) the seedlings are fit to be planted in secondary beds. Secondary bed sites are cleared of all growth and the weeds are uprooted. Disc plowing is done up to a depth of 30cm. The site is then levelled and 10m x 10m beds are formed. Six-month-old seedlings are planted at an espacement of 25 cm x 25 cm in the field.

Before planting the beds are flood watered. After planting flood watering should be done twice a week for one month. Thereafter, flood watering should be done once a week. After three months, one lime dressing - a dusting of lime powder over the beds is essential. This may be done before planting the bulbils in the primary beds as well as before planting the seedlings in the secondary beds. This helps in preventing the fungal attack. Instead of dusting calcium powder, calcium hydroxide solution also may be sprayed over the beds. Weeding should be done twice a month. DAP fertilizer may also be applied. After one year, the seedlings are ready for transplantation in the field.

9. Tropical Wild Almond Tree

(Published in "The Hindu . on the GARDENING page")

WHILE walking inside Anna University campus or on the way to IIT, Chennai, during January- February, one can see red blossoms hanging gracefully from tall majestic umbrella-like shaded trees. A close look will soon confirm that they are the large attractive fruits, not the flowers.

Botanically, the tree is known as *Sterculia foetida*; the wild almond or jungle badam tree was first observed and described by Linnaeus, a botanist in 1753. The flowers have a strong offensive smell when they appear in March. Hence the species is called S. foetida.

It belongs to the large family of Sterculiaceae and the genus Sterculia having 200 species of trees and shrubs found throughout the tropics, reaching its best development in tropical Asia. About 20 species are found in India.

It is a large, straight deciduous tree resembling *Bombax ceiba* in general appearance, with branches arranged in whorls and spreading horizontally. It attains a height of up to 40 meters and a girth of five meters.

New leaves appear in March-April and after flowering in March, the fruit ripens nearly 11 months after the flowers appear. It grows in the plains and the hills along the West coast from Kankan southwards up to an elevation of 800 meters. It is cultivated in gardens in several parts of India. Outside India, it is fairly distributed in tropical East Africa, Sri Lanka, Bangladesh, Malaysia, Burma, and North Australia.

The timber is greyish, white and soft. It is easy to saw and work on and fairly durable for interior work. It is used locally for dug-outs, boat planking, carved toys, and rough packing cases.

The bark yields a fiber suitable for ropes and exudes a gun. The seeds contain fixed oil 40 percent and starch. They have a pleasant taste and are eaten sometimes after roasting. Oil is extracted by boiling the seeds in water. The oil is a mild laxative and is used as a carminative. A decoction of fruit is mucilaginous and astringent.

The leaves are repellent and aperient. It is one of the fastest-growing species. It needs plenty of light, space, and loamy soil with enough moisture for its optimum development. For artificial reproduction seeds can be collected from ripened fruits (turned red to black) soon after their denizening in trees.

The viability of the seed is poor. Hence nursery can be raised in poly bags in the same year during March-April. Seedlings grow rapidly forming long tap roots and they can be planted with the onset of monsoon without much difficulty. It is one of the good avenue trees which can be planted for aesthetic purposes.

10. ROHIDA, the Drought- Resistant PLANT

(Published in The Science Express ... on the NATURE page)

Apart from being a great survivor, Rohida's brilliant colors make it a highly prized ornamental shrub.

ROHIDA, botanically known as *Tecomella undulata* or *Tecoma undulata*, is a deciduous ornamental shrub. Mostly grown in gardens for its handsome pale yellow to deep orange flowers, it is called Roheda in Hindi and Kutashalmali in Sanskrit.

The plant is also grown along roadsides, parks, and near public buildings. It grows in dry regions of the country like Rajasthan, Punjab, Gujarat and outer Himalaya.

A member of the Bignoniaceae family, the plant is a large shrub with drooping branches and greyish-green foliage, but when cultivated, it may grow as high as 12 meters with a girth of up to 2.4 m with good foliage serving as a shade tree. Leaves are oblong or linear-oblong.

From December to April, the tree is a delight to watch due to its orange flowers, arranged in a few lowered corymbose, racemes, on short lateral branches. Capsules 15-20 cm long, slightly curved, and smooth become ripe during May and July. Seeds are winged. The tree exudes gum from its bark.

The species is recommended for afforestation in dry areas of India, where rainfall is below 40 cm. It is an ideal species for dune stabilization, both for inland areas and coastal areas. And forest fire-prone arid zones and rain shadow zones of the Deccan peninsula. The plant is an excellent avenue tree for its graceful attractive flowers.

It can be propagated from either seeds or cuttings. In Tamil Nadu, the plant has been successfully grown in Sankaran Koil (Tirunelveli district) and Kudiraimozhi Theri (Tuthukudi district). It is fire-resistant. In north India, cattle browse it readily, but in Tamil Nadu, it has been observed that it is not generally browsed by cattle.

The plant's wood is tough, strong, durable, mottled, and handsome and is highly- prized for furniture, carvings, and agricultural implements. The bark of the young branches is used in the treatment of eczema and other medicinal purposes.

11. Tree Species with Potential

(Published in THE HINDU... on the GARDENING page)

At first sight one may think it is a drumstick or some other vegetable, looking at the elongated fruits of Rhizophora — a genus of mangrove forest on the seashore of tropics and subtropics.

Pods of *Rhizophora mucronata* look like drumstick

In Tamil, it is called Kandal, available mainly in the Pichavaram mangrove forests. In India, two common species are *Rhizophora mucronata* and *Rhizophora apiculata*. Both species grow six to 12 (15) m. tall along backwater canals and creeks. They are locally abundant in the Andaman and Nicobar Islands, the Sundarbans (West Bengal and Bangladesh), and in Pichavaram (Tamil Nadu coastline). They form impenetrable barriers by the stilt roots extruding from the trunk of the tree and sloping outwards and downwards to the mud bed protecting the land from coastal erosion.

The species look alike but there are differences. One is the leaf color *Rhizophora apiculata* whose leaves are dark green while *Rhizophora mucronata* has light green leaves and comparatively smaller ovoid fruit. They occur in tropical Southeast Asia, Sri Lanka, Africa, Madagascar, the Seychelles, Mauritius, and North Australia. A few robust trees of a hybrid variety, called *R. lamarcki* can be seen in Pichavaram.

The timber and logs are used for construction and making tool handles, posts, etc. The bark of Rhizophora is one rich and cheap source of tannin (25 to 40 percent) and is often used in the leather industry. The bark is a powerful astringent in the treatment of hemorrhage and angina. It is also used as a cure for diabetes.

It is estimated that the mangrove forests in the Sunderbans and the Andaman and Nicobar Islands together can yield annually about 132,000 tons of bark and 6.60 lakh tons of wood, indicating its potential to replace all the wattle and quebracho extract at present imported.

Rhizophora protects the seashore from sea swells, high-velocity gales, and cyclones. It grows on the outer fringe of the coastland and creeks and acts as a battalion to the sea shore acting as an interface between land and sea and arresting excessive inundation of land by seawater. Rhizophora along with other mangrove species with their highly developed and closely-knit root systems, work as natural filters and prevent erosion and loss of soil fertility during heavy rains and flash floods.

The seeds germinate when the fruit is still on the tree. On falling from the tree, the seedlings grow in the shallow water; Both the species give plenty of fruit in two distinct seasons. The fruit of *R. apiculata* is in July and October and *R. mucronata* in August and January. Within two or three months, the fruits become mature and they are collected to raise nurseries in polybags (15 cm x 25 cm) to facilitate artificial reproduction. The seedlings are planted along the banks of creeks or canals. Seedlings planted in canals dug out a year before planting give better results than planting in freshly created canals.

Experiments for artificial reproduction of Rhizhopora and other mangrove species are being done by the Tamil Nadu Forest Department and by the M. S. Swaminathan Research Foundation, Chennai, by making furrows and ridges in the mangrove forest areas in the State. The results were found to be encouraging for taking up large-scale planting.

12. The Changing Face of Conservation

(Published in THE HINDU on the Sunday page)

Today, if the concept of conservation of biodiversity is to become meaningful, policies must take into account local participation and cultural factors. This is imperative with a celebration of International Day for Biological Diversity

ASIA harbors an enormous diversity of plant and animal species. The region is also home to some of the oldest cultures, where ancient wisdom has valued the conservation of nature for the benefit of mankind.

December 29 is International Day for Biological Diversity which commemorates the implementation of the International Convention on Biological Diversity. The term "biological diversity" refers to life in its entirety, which includes microorganisms, plants, and animals. According to the Forest Survey of India report, 1997, the country lost 5,500 km. of forest-cover sq. k in 1977. The total forest area is estimated at 63.34 million hectares, which is 19.27 percent of the total land area. India is believed to rank sixth- among 12 Mega Bio diverse countries. Our range of bio-diversity is unique due to a varied physical environment.

Starting from World Environment Day, Vana Mahotsav, and World Forestry Day . on the lines of seminars, conventions, and treaties at the national and world bio-zonal levels, several treaties, based on the highest and most ideal objectives, have been committed. But how successful have we been?

In 1925 the first speaker at the 50th anniversary of the American Forestry Association said that while the topic was on 50 years of conservation it might as well have been called 50 years of the levels of conversation.

In India, despite stringent forest legislation, a carefully crafted forest policy, and treaties, covering basic objectives, we have still to accept the fact that conservation is at a crossroads. In this context, I recall Clemenceau's phrase:

"War is too serious a matter to be left to professional soldiers". The responsibility to conserve bio-diversity is too big a job and too important in its implications to be left to professional foresters but wait a moment.

What would have happened had it been under the management of a few agricultural departments rather than a million productivity of the land?

There is an element of apprehension among ecologists that a significant proportion of diversity could be lost soon. Therefore, it is time that the environment same priority as food security for all, despite the principle of common but different responsibilities for protecting the environment or biodiversity we seem to lack the courage to act upon this and take it to its logical conclusion.

Forestry has been practiced with different objectives, and, accordingly, termed differently protection, production, farm, and social forestry. With a gradual management change in attitude and experiences, joint forest management is changing.

The aim is to involve local people. At this initial stage, people's participation is directed by bureaucrats and executives.

The next step is still awaited when local committees will decide their priorities and the mode of operation in forestry and environment protection activities. The environment cannot be an issue for the government alone. It has to be a mass movement. Reviewing the role of cultural and emotional sentiments, deeply ingrained amongst our people are the examples of the sacred groves, and the *Sthala Vriksha* (temple trees). Sacred groves occur in almost all parts of rural India. In villages, sacred groves occur around places of worship Around the village deities are small groves of naturally growing species. These are regarded as sacred as the deities themselves and are free of interference.

It has been recorded by a study group that such groves in Andhra Pradesh have, on average. more than 134 rare and endemic plants. They are repositories of rare and valuable flora and fauna. Could this instance of cultural forestry suggest any better alternative strategy for the preservation of our valuable genome? These areas of cultural heritage, and ecological and sociological information need to be tended.

The initiative taken by the Karnataka Forest Department to encourage the preservation of bio-diversity under the names Navagraha Vana, Nakshatra Vana, and Dhanwanti Vana (for medicinal plants) seems to be much more appealing in terms of impressing upon us the need for conservation. The ideals of conserving or maintaining sacred groves, *sthala vrikshas*, (temple trees), and raising medicinal plant plots viz Dhanvantari Vana can be anticipated as the most effective mode to conserve the diverse biota involving local people.

Every year, under joint forestry management, hundreds of program villages are allotted simple funds, an objective being to conserve biodiversity in the area. The National Forest Policy of India. Agenda 21 of the Rio de Janeiro (1992) Declaration emphasizes the participation of women in their environment. Unfortunately, women remain at the lowest rung in the context of environmental protection due to serious gender inequality in every sphere of society. They remain half-wage earners for a whole day of drudgery. This negative bias is so strong at the various levels that despite proper legislation the legitimate rights of women in a simple issue could not be protected. The National Education Policy and Agenda 21 stress environmental education being imparted at even the elementary stage of education.

Accordingly, this has been introduced in the syllabi. Schoolchildren do learn: what a forest is. about soil erosion, soil conservation, and other aspects of the environment. But can they identify soil erosion or the few plants they come across every day? How many children can imagine a forest without having seen or been to a forest area? Barring the people living in and around forests, most people do not know a thing about our forests. Many have never been to a jungle. There are others too who will never see a forest in their lifetime. This type of apathy towards conservation has resulted in a lack of synergy towards fostering a love for nature.

During ceremonial functions commemorating various international days like World Environment Day and World Forestry Day, children are asked to raise slogans like "We shall plant trees and get rain". In a tree planting ceremony in Chennai, school children at the function were rehearsing a slogan to be chanted loudly as soon as the chief guest came.

This is an example of a mechanical system for students. No child has the basic idea of nurturing a plant. The average school, when it can afford to, establishes a computer lab but not a nursery. It is time we are required to ponder over these issues and implement our policies at the grassroots level based on our cultural background.

13. The Sacking Tree

(Published in the Science Express—on the NATURE page)

By Manoj Kumar Sarcar & Dr Aruna Basu Sarcar

THE Upas tree, the largest south India species, is popularly called 'the sacking tree' because its fibers are used for making sacks.

Known as *Jasund* or *Jungli Lkuch* in Hindi, as *Valkala* in Sanskrit and as *Marauri* or *Aranthelli* in Tamil, Upas reaches heights up to 78 metres and 4.8 metres girth, with a straight cylindrical bole; found in the moist deciduous forests of Western Ghats and Andaman islands.

female flowers are solitary. Fig like purple or crimson velvetty fruits are single seeded and immensely bitter.

The bark can be readily stripped off in large pieces, soaked in water and beaten well to extract white and furry fibres. These fibres from inner bark are strong and tenacious and suitable

The seeds are extracted after cleaning the pulp and dried in shade. Germination percentage is about 90 per cent. Seeds are to be collected during November-January. Sowing the seeds within one month after collection gives better results.

If leaf-litter is added to the mother

The Upas tree, the largest south Indian species, is popularly called 'the sacking tree' because its fibers are used for making sacks.

Botanically, Upas is known as *Antiaris toxicaria* and belongs to the family Moraceae. The species name toxicaria suggests the toxic nature of the plant. When the stem is pierced, a milky sap exudes which forms a thick brown resinous gum after drying. This is the celebrated arrow poison, Upas Antiaris, used to b poison arrows in Java, Malaysia, and Burma. However, such extremely toxic properties are not found in trees growing in India and Ceylon.

Known as Jasund or Jungli-Lkuch in Hindi, as Valkala in Sanskrit, and as Marauri or Aranthelli in Tamil, Upas reaches heights up to 76 meters and 4.8 meters girth, with a straight cylindrical bole; found in the moist deciduous forests of the Western Ghats and Andaman Islands.

In Tamil Nadu, it is found in the forests of Coimbatore district. Recently, this tree of 5.2-meter girth has been discovered at the Five Falls area in Courtallam, Tirunelveli district. Similarly, six more trees were found growing near Forest Rest house at Courtallam.

This huge tree, trunk often buttressed, has brownish grey smooth bark, leaves 10-20 cm long, oblong or elliptic, glossy, base cordate. Male flowers are found on the surface of an orbicular axillary receptacle, while female flowers are solitary. Fig-like purple or crimson velvety fruits are single-seeded and immensely bitter.

The bark can be readily stripped off in large pieces, soaked in water, and beaten well to extract white and furry fibers. These fibres from inner bark are strong tenacious and suitable for cordage and matting. The wood is suitable for packing cases, matchboxes, splints, and for paper pulp. The latex or the milky vicious sap, which, exudes from the stem owes its poisonous property to the presence of the chemical components antiarin and antiarin. The toxicity of the latex varies according to edaphic and climatic conditions. In the Konkan and Canara, the bitter seeds are used as a febrifuge and to treat dysentery, one-third to one-half of a seed is given three times a day.

The seeds are extracted after cleaning the pulp and dried in shade. The germination percentage is about 80 percent. Seeds are to be collected during November-January. Sowing the seeds within one month after collection gives better results.

If leaf litter is added to the mother bed, germination occurs much faster. Usually, eight-month-old seedlings can be pricked out (approximately 40-50 cm tall) and can be planted at specific planting sites. Upas trees are ideal for altitudes above 200 meters, especially in the Western Ghats, where soil moisture is ensured. It is also an ideal tree for carrying out plantation work to enrich the bio-diversity of the forests, being with the graceful status, as the largest tree in south India.

14. Robust Shrub

(Published in THE HINDU on the GARDENING page)

The Ringworm Cassia or the Candle Bush plant, a robust shrub that grows up to two meters is a native of South America. When in bloom it attracts passers-by with its foliage and golden yellow flowers. It grows wild near cultivated lands and along water courses and is also grown as a garden plant.

As the name suggests Ringworm Cassia is useful for curing skin diseases. In Sanskrit, it is known as Dadhrugna in Hindi and Bengali, Dadhmardan, suggesting its usefulness in curing ringworm disease. In Tamil, it is known as Seemayiagatthi. The plant belongs to the Caesalpiniaceae family.

The branches are thick, leaves sub-sessile, glandless, 30-60 cm long with persistent stipules and leaflets 8-12 pairs. The flowers bloom during November-February in dense erect paniculate racemes.

The pods are 10-20 cm long, having margins with two longitudinal crenulate wings. The seeds are flattened, triangular, and about 50 or more in number in a pod. The pods appear during December.

The plant possesses various medicinal values. The fresh leaf juice or the decoction of the leaf or the flowers is a remedy for skin diseases like herpes, ringworm, and itches. The decoction of the leaves and flowers is used in curing bronchitis, asthma, and in stomatitis.

The leaves are insecticidal. A strong decoction of flowers or roots are good lotion for rheumatism. The roots are of a mild purgative nature. The plant can also be used for green manure in areas, where acidic soil is not suitable for the use of chemical fertilizers.

The ripened pods can be collected from January to March. The black-colored mature seeds are sown on raised mother-beds formed by sandy loam soil as soon as the seedlings become 2-3 cm in size, they are transplanted in small polythene bags.

When the seedlings become 25-30 cm tall, they can be planted at desired places. The plant requires bright sunshine and sufficient soil moisture to grow well. The Foundation for Revitalization of Local Health Traditions (FRLHT) Bangalore. is making efforts to propagate such medicinal plants through their Medicinal Plants Conservation Network (MPCN) in Tamil Nadu, Karnataka, and Kerala.

PART IV: REAL STORIES OF ILLEGAL GANJA CULTIVATION IN FORESTS

15. Destructions of Ganja (*Cannabis sativa*) Cultivation Plants in Western Ghats

*C*annabis sativa* is an annual herbaceous flowering plant. The species was first classified by Carl Linnaeus in 1753. It has been cultivated throughout recorded history and used as a source of industrial fiber, seed oil, food, and medicine. It is also used as a recreational drug and for religious and spiritual purposes.

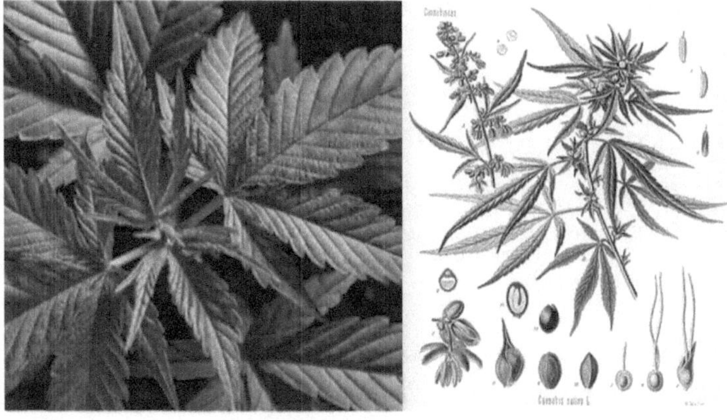

Marijuana refers to the leaves and flowering portions of cannabis when used as a drug, intoxicant, or medicine.

Cannabis sativa is the most common type of cannabis plant used as marijuana. Marijuana is primarily smoked or ingested orally when used for its psychoactive effects.

The primary psychoactive constituent of marijuana is a cannabinoid, delta-9-tetrahydrocannabinol (THC), which produces relaxation, mild euphoria, sedation, and perceptual distortion.

Cannabis sativa is known among many cultures for its medicinal potential. C. sativa has been used for the treatment of rheumatism, epilepsy, asthma, skin burns, pain, the management of sexually transmitted diseases, difficulties during child labor, and gastrointestinal activity. However, the use of C. sativa is still limited, and it is illegal in most countries.

The 1961 international treaty Single Convention on Narcotic Drugs classed cannabis with hard drugs. During the negotiations, the Indian delegation opposed its intolerance to the social and religious customs of India and banned its illegal cultivation. But it is illegally cultivated by a group of greedy people inside the forest areas that are mostly inaccessible to earn quick money.

The present story is based on a real incident that happened in one of the reserved forests in the Western Ghat area of Tirunelveli district.

I was then in full charge of District Forest Officer of Tirunelveli district –a district located down south of Tamil Nadu just before Kanyakumari district. A large extent of this district falls in the southern part of Western Ghats where four Forest Ranges are situated from south to north namely Courtrallam, Kadayanallur, Puliangudi, and Sivagiri for the protection of forest resources and administration.

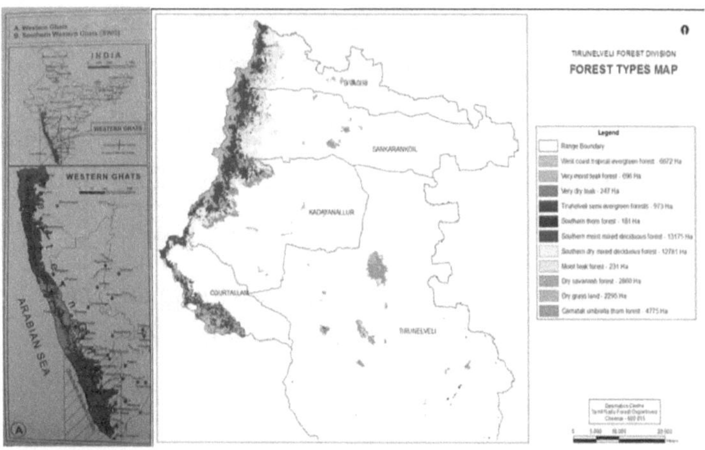

Maps showing the Western Ghats and the Tirunelveli Forest division

In the eastern part of the Western Ghats, lies Tamil Nadu while Kerala is situated in the western part of the Western Ghats (add map). The Western Ghats Mountain starts from Kanyakumari – the southernmost district of Tamil Nadu and goes up to 1600 km towards the north crossing Karnataka, Maharashtra, and Goa then up to Saurashtra of Gujarat. That means all along the great Arabian Sea on the western side, this Western Ghats is decorated with rich Forest cover, verities of beautiful birds and animals, enchanting rivers and streams, and the mosaics of human settlements of our country.

As a whole the Western Ghats endows a remarkable biodiversity, and gives a serene and beautiful natural look that attracts a large number of tourists throughout the year. It attracted me too many times to go there and get the green bathing. On many occasions, we used to go in jeep up to the last point of a motorable road then we carry our ration items, a few utensils, and lightweight tents for night halt.

Of course, the team would be composed of a few security staff with guns and ammunition. There would not be any well-marked paths in forests or to climb up the higher altitudes.

Therefore, it would be a trek to reach a safe destination near some natural water body for pitching our tents. The Agasthiyamalai biosphere reserve and its peak (1889m) are located on the Tamil Nadu and Kerala border in southern Western Ghats. The locality is very beautiful with rich flora and fauna. It is also the cultural home of Siddha. We made challenging trekking there but were not able to come back to plain land in the same night... a very thrilling story that we dealt with separately. This is the first part of the present story.

After attending office work at Kokkirakulam on the bank of Tambroparni and having a discussion with the district Collector, I was late to come back home- a hundred years old bungalows constructed in 1900 AD during the conservator of forests revered Hassan Saheb.

Afternoon, I did not go to the office, attending to the important files in the camp office. Suddenly I received a call from an unknown number stating "Sir I am speaking from Puliangudi, in your Velladu Saragam Ganja cultivation is going on, and plants are growing, take immediate action". The entire message was in Tamil. Then there was no sound after this message. After my repeated efforts, I could not contact him nor could I find out to check the veracity of this message.

I had a good rapport with common people and many times, they provided me with good feedback and truthful messages. Further, from the voice tone of the messenger, I decided to go to the field with full preparation. It was the evening of 14/ 15 January 1999. The PONGAL festival (offering of new rice and vegetables to the Sun God) is completed all over Tamil Nadu when people enjoy their cake of new rice, and green vegetables after offering and worshiping the SUN God in gratitude. We too celebrated the same in front of our bungalow at Tirunelveli.

After getting the one-line message, I thought deeply about every petty thing in preparation to make it a successful raid without disclosing any information to anybody. A group of people kept eyes always about the movement of us. However, I just asked my driver casually whether my vehicle had sufficient oil, etc. He replied everything was fit for the move at any time. My driver Mr. Ramakrishna was a very faithful man, dependable clever, and used to take care of the safety of the officer. I informed him to come prepared to stay in a camp for two days and report tonight at 12-30 am. Besides, I informed Mr. Chintamather, Range Officer Kadayanallur to come to readiness at Kadayanallur forest rest house at 2 am along with a Forester and security staff with their weapons. I also talked to ROs, Courtrallam, Forest station Senkotta, Sankarankoil (Puliangudi), and Sivagiri with a similar message to reach Kadayanallur rest house at two am. With full preparation. However, I did not disclose the things to be done, where, when, or any other details of my plan. Only all were informed to come prepared at 2 am at Kadayanallur rest house.

Ramakrishna came to my camp office in time and kept the vehicle ready in front of the house. I kept myself ready in advance and did not forget to take my revolver. At 01:15 am, we started for Kadayanallur rest house. Ramakrishna was driving the jeep very fast but the steady, road was free from traffic. We reached the rest house at 2:05 am. Mr. Chindamather RO was standing in full uniform along with his forester and security staff. I have not told you anything about the program. Informed him to keep ready certain materials and come back at 2-30am. The other 4 ROs reached at 2:30 am in uniform with their security staff.

I did not sleep. Thoroughly studied the S.O.I Topographical sheet to find out the exact location of Velladu Saragam, its distance from the foothills, and assessed the approximate time to reach there and how much altitude we need to climb. With my assessment, I understood that at around 3 am if we start it would be correct to reach the site just at the daybreak with the Sunlight. We had a closed-door meeting with ROs for a few minutes, briefed them, and told them to follow my vehicle. At 3-20 am we started.

Ramakrishna was in front and leading to the place that I indicated to him earlier. Other vehicles of Range officers were following with security and supporting staff. We were proceeding north on the main road at a slow speed. After about 20 km, we reached Puliangudi then moved west on a semi-kachcha road and reached the foothills of the Western Ghats, altitude of about 330 m. around 4 am. It was still dark, could not find any settlement nearby. All of us took our bags containing requirements during trekking from the vehicles.

Security Guards carried their weapons. Drivers were instructed to be in vehicles keeping light in deem mode.

We started from the foothills at about 4-15 am. We have to trek and climb up about 550 meters hereafter to reach Vellangudi Saragam. After reaching a small distance, we stopped for a while and I briefed all ROs and their staff with special tips to security guards. The purpose of my plan was yet to be disclosed. Tamil Nadu Government allowed the recruitment of local hill tribal boys in the Forest Department. In all 4 ranges of the Western Ghats of Tirunelveli district also recruited about a dozen forest guards/forest watchers as forefront protection staff. These boys were quite faithful through all the hilly tracks.

I called Ratnam - a young tribal watcher of the Puliyangudi range to come in front of me and navigate the path to reach Velladu Saragam before Sunrise. Ratnam along with my security guard were moving fast to our destination. After trekking about 500 meters, we found a small hilly tributary. Crossed the shallow water after keeping the hunter's shoe in hand. From our whispering and the sound of crossing water bodies, a group of dogs started burking. Ratnam informed me that a small hamlet of the Kanni tribe is located just near this tributary. A few tribal women came forward to stop their dogs from burking. Anyway, within 3 to 4 minutes, we crossed the hamlet, but the wave of sound of dogs was floating in our ears.

After trekking for about one and a half hours, we reached the Vellangudi Saragam. In the torchlight, I confirmed that we were almost near the place where Ganja cultivation is expected. After trekking for another 5 to 6 minutes daylight flashes in our eyes. I called all members of the group and dared to disclose that there was an illegal Ganja cultivation field nearby. I again addressed them, that all be careful with self-protection and the group and find out this field. RO Puliyangudi and his concerned staff were scared as this area comes under their administrative jurisdiction. Soon after crossing a small ridge, we found the Ganja field. It was a very tricky, sloppy land, almost an inaccessible place. To avoid a fall, cautioned the group to enter the field very carefully taking support each other.

With the proper signal, I indicated all security guards and ROs to keep the weapons in readiness and we entered the Ganja field. It was a quite large area, maybe a half of an acre. The small seedling was planted, maybe by the end of November or in the early part of December of last year taking advantage of northeast monsoon rain. Thank God, none was there in the field. That was a great escape as these criminals (or their owners) used to invest a large chunk of money to grow these 6 months crops to get higher returns in a short time. Therefore, they take full protection and do not hesitate to fire if any person enters that field. We were a group of 24, so chances would have been more to be affected as victims by these criminals. There was a big-sized naked rock or huge boulder. The criminals made shelter behind this rock, kept their utensils, and made a sort of ad hock kitchen. We could notice raw rice, salt small onions, dry chilly, and a few polyethylene bags, etc.

The Station RO told Sir, we must be very careful; these fellows normally would not leave such a field without keeping some protection measure. He did even not complete his sentence; someone fired us, which hit that huge rock. We kept each of us in protected places and noticed that downside some 4 to 5 men were coming towards this field with big packets on their heads. In return, the Station range officer noticed them and fired at once, the other two security Guards also fired them. The criminals run away downside to escape and save their lives by throwing their head loads. Thank God, we all escaped from the shootings of the criminals. Three guards and station RO with guns went down and checked the gunny bags thrown and escaped by the criminals. Bags were full of rice, vegetables sugar, pickles, fertilizer, and dress materials. They were coming back to the Ganja field after celebrating their traditional festivals -the Pongal at their native places. They never thought that anybody could reach such a remote, inaccessible place so early in the morning. It is also to be thought of that what could have been our fate, had it been they reached just 15 -20 minutes before us!

We all were exhausted and took some rest for a while, keeping security alert by two Guards. Ratnam came near and handed over a bag given by Ramakrishna -my driver to him at the foothills. I was surprised and happy to see the Tajmahal dip tea bag of 25, unopened, biscuit packets and paper cups. What a great joy! All of us had tea as amrita(nectar)! Joy Ramakrishna whose presence of mind and services I always enjoyed. Our fatigue withered and we started uprooting Ganja plants, which accumulated in heaps at various sites and burnt into ashes using petrol. Used paper cups for tea were also burnt. There was a long plastic black pipe for supplying water to the plants to avoid casualties and their faster growth. Sufficient photographs were taken of the Ganja plants, field materials available there for their use, etc., and also the scene of burning the plants.

Uprootal, collection, and burning of Ganja plants in the Western Ghats area by field staff

Near the big boulder that they were using as their kitchen, we received an invitation card near the sugar packet addressed to a political man of the present running govt from Puliyangudi.

Many prim facie pieces of evidence were available with this invitation card. Along with this and in corroboration with other links, it could be ascertained that this person was involved with this illegal activity in the reserved forest area of the Puliangudi range of this district.

The maghazer (list of pieces of evidence found in the field during the operation of illegal Ganja cultivation inside the forests) was prepared with all details of materials found there; this invitation card was also attached to this maghazer.

It was about 8-30 am on 16 January 1999. All of us were very hungry and tired. We checked everything before leaving the place. We slowly climbed up to the normal place from where we entered the illegally cultivated Ganja field.

We took the same trekking path we followed during the night to reach the field. Quickly we reached the same tribal hamlet then to the foothills finally to the Puliyangudi range office. Some idlis were arranged for all as breakfast from the nearby hotel. Soon after finishing, breakfast RO, Puliyangudi and RO Forest station, Senkottha with sufficient force (Foresters and Forest guards) arrested the main culprit in Puliyangudi and took in front of the Judicial Magistrate, Puliyangudi Session court with all pieces of evidence. The Judicial Magistrate ordered him for 7 days under judicial custody.

I was about to move to Tirunelveli, my HQ, when I just received a mobile call "Manoj, (I am...) speaking from Chennai, are you sure that one of my party men is involved in Ganja cultivation in the forest area in Puliangudi range?" Without any second thought, I just replied, "Vanakkam Sir, it is true, and I was in the field to lead the Ganja eviction team. This person was directly involved in this illegal activity." "Okay go ahead" – that was the instant replay of the then honorable forest minister of the State Government.

Certainly, it was a great surprise and fearlessness for me now when the honorable minister directly asked me that you arrest my party man, and ordered me to go ahead. In fact, in that period taking action against the party man of the running govt. by a govt servant, it goes directly against the individual. Even he can expect immediate transfer or get some disciplinary case against him under some pretext or other. However, here in this case it was altogether different. Not only I was told to go ahead but the honorable minister informed the Chief Minister not to allow the alleged person into the CM's residence or in office.

This was a successful operation in evicting the illegal Ganja cultivation with point-to-point systematic planning and efforts of all Range officers and other field staff. More satisfaction was there as the govt supported the action of an officer and his staff. This gave us further confidence to carry out the work fearlessly keeping our honesty and self-dignity close to our hearts.

PART V: HOW WE CAN LIVE LONG LIKE TREES

16. Oldest Trees of the World and How One Becomes Immortal

Our Average life expectancy varies from 60 to 80 years. For a few, it may cross even a hundred or a few more years but not comparable with the average life expectancy of trees. Here is a list of tree species that even sustained more than 1000 years, or even more. A shortlist of such trees is available from all over the world whose life expectancy was estimated to vary more than 5000 to 10000 years. Here is the list of a few trees.

The ages of these trees are estimates and subject to revision as more accurate dating methods are developed. Here are a few examples:

1. The General Sherman Tree (*Sequoia sempervirens*) Redwoods. About 2,000 years old and is a giant among giants. Located in Sequoia National Park, USA	**2. The Largest & Oldest Teak tree (*Tectona grandis*) in the World:** Estimated Age: Maybe 4000 years? at Parambikulam Tiger Reserve, Kerala, seen in June 2012. This Great Teak Tree is 39.98M in height & is 7.02M at GBH as measured during 1994-95. The Tree is declared as " Mahavriksha" by Govt of India.
3. Bristlecone Pine (*Pinus longaeva*): **Name: Methuselah**	**4. Giant Sequoia (*Sequoiadendron giganteum*):** Name: Prometheus (formerly)

Location: White Mountains, California, USA Estimated Age: Over 4,800 years	Location: Wheeler Peak, Nevada, USA (destroyed in 1964) Estimated Age: Over 4,900 years (before its destruction)
5. Yew (*Taxus baccata*): **Name: Llangernyw Yew** Location: Conwy, Wales Estimated Age: Over 4,000 to 5,000 years	**6. Olive Tree (Olea europaea):** **Name: Olive Tree of Vouves** Location: Crete, Greece Estimated Age: Over 2,000 to 3,000 years
7. Baobab (Adansonia): **Name: Panke Baobab** Location: Maun, Botswana (collapsed in 2017) Estimated Age: Over 6,000 years (before its collapse)	**8. Sugi (Cryptomeria japonica):** **Name: Jomon Sugi** Location: Yakushima, Japan Estimated Age: Over 2,170 to 7,200 years
9.Quaking Aspen (Populus tremuloides): **Name: Pando** Location: Fishlake National Forest, Utah, USA Estimated Age: Over 80,000 years (though Pando is a clonal colony, and individual stems may not be as old)	

Many of us will be interested to know how it happens. How do the trees of the plant community live for such long periods?

A few reasons may be as follows which may be Stunning learning for all of us

1. The trees follow the theory of expanding their love through their continuous supply of food and live air and consuming the exogenous flow of carbon dioxide by themselves. That is the theory of taking the position of a giver to all, but not expecting anything in return. They are originally the renunciant, the Great Monks.

2. They are not greedy like us as we everything like to take in our possession irrespective of what sufficient we have.

3. The finding of the knitting of the root system of redwood - The Sequoia on the east coast of California is still surprising. I quote from a speech delivered by one of the monks in America.

"A few years ago, I was walking with a friend in the Muir Woods, which is just close to San Francisco It's a redwood forest. We came upon a park ranger; He was explaining to some tourists the secret of the forest. He said that the Sequoia or Redwood trees (Sequoia sempervirans) are the largest trees on the planet. Some of them are hundreds or even thousands of years old. But interestingly, their roots do not grow deep and then he said that these trees have been saved for centuries and centuries, enduring massive wind storms, frigid blizzards, and devastating earthquakes. And without deep roots, how do they keep standing? Then the Ranger paused so that we could ponder this will start to reveal to us the underground secret movement for history. And being from the 60s I like underground things. So, I was very attempting. He said that the roots under the ground reach outward seeking the roots of other Redwood trees. And when

they meet, they intertwine, making a permanent bond with each other. In this way, all the Redwood trees in the entire forest are either directly or indirectly giving support to each other Unity is their strength. They reach out to care for each other. Even the little newborn baby red ones, their little, tiny boots are given shelter by the ancient Giants in the Mill Woods, nature has given humanity a very crucial lesson. There is real strength in our willingness to care for and support each other. They'll be takers of dividing property Wisdom is to understand the simple, universal principle that you're giving receive by getting things by giving. We make a life The spiritual evolution of a society can be understood when people love people and use things. But, all too often, in today's world, it's just the opposite People use people and they love things."

We need to live together, knitting with each other, and extending health to each other as redwoods do this. But today, in contrast, we never leave the war with lethal weapons causing suffering and death of our fellow human beings. Plants never do this kind of genocide. They even help and allow the smaller plants to grow under their shades with good health.

4. Of course, they do not have the vocal cords like us to shout, but they communicate to the aspirants through their subtle voice to help them I could listen to that intuitively and benefited many times as mentioned in my first book "Self-Mastery, and Enlightenment through the Kingdom of plants".

5. Many other extraordinary qualities help them to survive. To survive more than thousands of years even on their

death and decade condition, they nourished the soil to be fertile, to grow our food crops.

6. All these are the lessons and learning messages for human beings, and at least after going through these books, we take the vows that save the greens. We carry forward action taking care of this benevolent living entity. We survive for more years to protect them and protect ourselves. I take the opportunity to example of the life of two trees. That is one of the oldest trees from India. The largest and the age-old tree is redwoods from the USA.

A). The Largest & Oldest Teak tree (*Tectona grandis*) in the World:

The Largest & Oldest Teak tree (Tectona grandis) in the World at Parambikulam Tiger Reserve, Kerala, seen in June 2012. This Great Teak Tree is 39.98M in height & is 7.02M at GBH as measured during 1994-95. The Tree is declared as " Mahavriksha" by Govt of India. It remains our primary duty to protect and preserve this heritage living monument.

B) The General Sherman Tree (Sequoia sempervirens) is about 2,000 years old and is a giant among giants. The General Sherman Tree in Sequoia National Park:

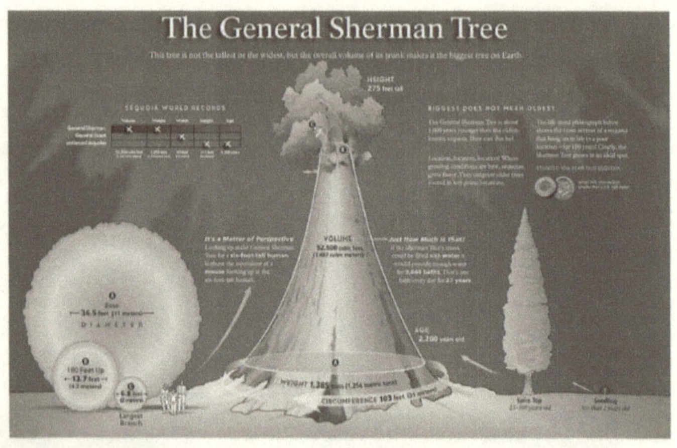

Author: Garrison Frost, joined Save the Redwoods League in 2019 as its Director of Communications.

When you spend your time talking about coast redwoods and giant sequoia, you get used to a different scale, a scale that is hard to reconcile with most other things in the forest.

But even for people who are conditioned to deal with BIG, the General Sherman Tree in Sequoia National Park is a whole different thing. Considered the world's largest tree, measured by volume, it stands 275 feet tall and is over 36 feet in diameter at the base. Sixty feet above the base, it is still 17.5 feet.

But throwing out numbers doesn't capture it. Photos don't give you a sense, because it's so big there's no way to get a decent picture of it. Perhaps this will help: In 2006 a 98-foot-long branch fell off the tree. So, the Sherman Tree lost a branch the size of a huge tree ... and was fine!

The General Sherman Tree is about 2,000 years old and is a giant among giants. In a world full of threats and challenges, it has planted its roots and set its defenses. It is strong and ready.

Biology:

The coast redwood is one of the world's fastest-growing conifers or cone-bearing trees. In contrast to the tree's size, redwood cones are very small — only about an inch long.

Each cone contains a few dozen tiny seeds: it would take well over 100,000 seeds to weigh a pound! In good conditions, redwood seedlings grow rapidly, sometimes more than a foot annually.

Young trees also sprout from the base of their parent's trunk, taking advantage of the energy and nutrient reserves contained within the established root system.

Frequent, naturally occurring fires play an important role in maintaining coast redwood forests because they rid the forest floor of combustible materials.

Forest fires create space for redwood seedlings (and other plants) to grow. In contrast, decades of fire suppression practices usually result in the accumulation of dead plant material that may fuel intense, destructive fires.

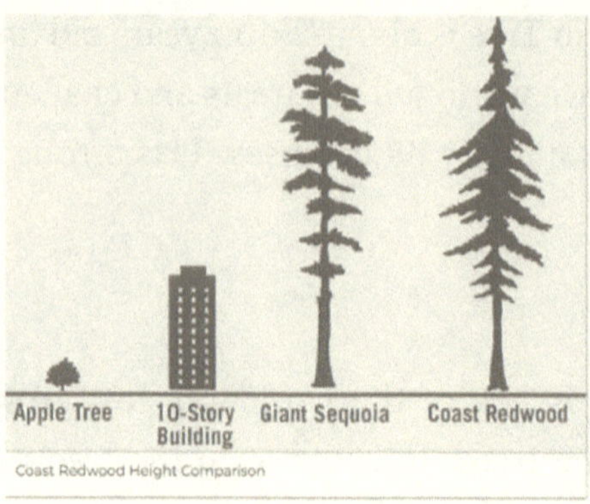

Coast Redwood Height Comparison

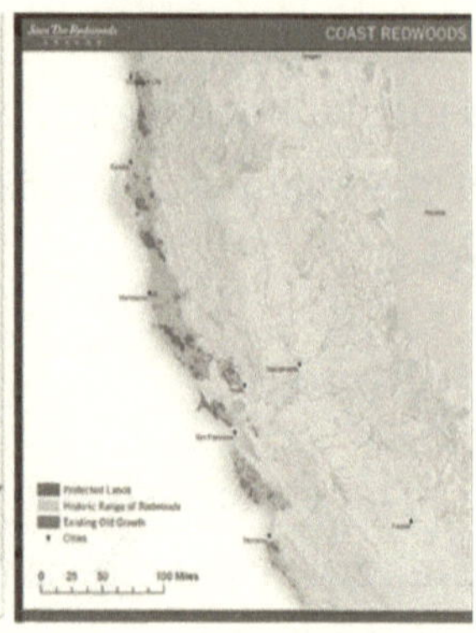

Frequent, naturally occurring fires play an important role in maintaining coast redwood forests because they rid the forest floor of combustible materials. Forest fires create space for redwood seedlings (and other plants) to grow. In contrast, decades of fire suppression practices usually result in the accumulation of dead plant material that may fuel intense, destructive fires.

Redwoods can usually survive natural forest fires because of their thick (up to 12 inches), protective bark. Redwoods get their name from the beautiful reddish hue of their bark. Redwood bark is soft, fibrous, and rich in tannins (which help prevent insect damage). You can learn more about the impact of fire on our redwood and sequoia forests through our blog.

Where coast redwoods live, temperatures are moderate year-round. Heavy rains provide the trees with much-needed water during the winter months and dense summer fog contributes moisture to the forest during the dry summer months. Redwoods even create their own "rain" by capturing fog on their leaves. The coastal fog condenses on redwood needles creating water droplets. Some of the water is absorbed by the needles and some drips to the ground, providing water to the redwood forest understory. You can learn more about the relationship of redwood forest plants and fog through our research grants.

In recent years, scientists have discovered that life abounds in the canopy (the tops of old trees) and on the forest floor. Canopy research supported by Save the Redwoods League has revealed that many species can live in the redwood canopy, including worms, salamanders, and plants such as Sitka spruce, ferns, and huckleberry.

Learn more about these majestic trees and download California's Redwood State Parks brochure.

Conservation:

Since 1918, Save the Redwoods League has been working to protect, restore, and conserve our remaining redwood forests. We have helped protect redwood forests and surrounding land totaling more than 200,000 acres (about the size of New York City).

Our conservation work depends on close partnerships with scientists, land managers, industries, and other land conservation organizations. We're the only organization with the type of comprehensive approach needed to ensure that forests that take one thousand years to grow will be here for another thousand years.

You can learn more about our conservation work by visiting our protect and restore pages.

Research:

To help protect redwood forests, we must continue to study them. There is still much we do not know about these towering giants and their surrounding forests. Through our Research Grants Program, we have learned that:

Redwood forests are affected by the tree disease commonly known as "sudden oak death." Sudden oak death kills Tanoak trees, a redwood forest inhabitant. When tanoaks die, extra brush is created, increasing fire intensity by three to four times than those in forests not affected by the disease.

Amphibian species are also affected by the destruction of old-growth forests. Researchers found fewer than half as many animals at a property containing young, very small, mostly second-growth trees than at adjacent parkland containing undisturbed forests.

To increase the population of martens, which depend on old-growth forests for their home, researchers found that suitable marten habitat can be created by planting understory shrubs like rhododendrons and evergreen huckleberries, strategically removing roads and installing "rest boxes" for the animals.

You can read more about League-funded research projects on our research grants page.

Redwoods and Climate Change Initiative:

To meet the pressing need for research on how redwoods can survive sweeping environmental changes, the League and

Redwoods scientists launched the multiyear Redwoods and Climate Change Initiative. Our goal is to create a comprehensive climate adaptation strategy for the redwoods. These findings will help focus League efforts on where to protect and restore redwood forestland according to climate change forecasts.

Working on scales from leaves to landscapes, no other team of investigators in the world has the unique and complementary skills to conduct this integrated 10-year investigation of redwoods. The investigation includes a network of forest plots that can be monitored for more than 100 years. This program will yield data-based solutions to protect redwoods in a changing world. Read about our initial results on our Understanding Climate Change pages.

17. Our Physical Body Dies, and The Soul (Part of Supreme Consciousness) Never perishes, and remains Eternally Living, Let Us Be in That

As per the sacred literature The Bhagavad Gita of Sanatana Dharma or Hinduism where in the battleground of Kurukshetra SriKrisna clearly stated about the perishable body and the nonperishable Soul, not the destructible Soul. These are narrated below

*The bodies are for the soul just like clothes are for us. Just as we discard worn garments the soul discards worn-out bodies and accepts new ones.

* The soul cannot be divided, burnt, dissolved, or dried up. It is eternal, all-pervading, unalterable, unmoving, and without a beginning.

*It is said that the self cannot be seen, understood, or changed. Knowing this you should not mourn for the body.

* Even if you believe that the soul is continually born and dies continually, you still do not have any reason to lament for it.

*Birth and death are unavoidable matters. Do not lament over them because those who are born will certainly die one day and those who die will be born again one day.

You are the original Personality of Godhead, the oldest, the ultimate sanctuary of the entire universe. You are the knower and the knowledge. The supreme abode. The entire universe is pervaded by you.

Sanskrit	English
वासांसि जीर्णानि यथा विहाय नवानि गृह्णाति नरोऽपराणि तथा शरीराणि विहाय जीर्णान्यन्यानि संयाति नवानि देही।	The bodies are for the soul just like clothes are for us. Just as we discard worn garments the soul discards worn-out bodies and accepts new ones. 2/22
नैनं छिन्दन्ति शस्त्राणि नैनं दहति पावकः। न चैनं क्लेदयन्त्यापो न शोषयति मारुतः।।	The self cannot be wounded by weapons, burned by fire, moistened by water, or blown away by wind. 2/23
अच्छेद्योऽयमदाह्योऽयमक्लेद्योऽशोष्य एव च। नित्यः सर्वगतः स्थाणुरचलोऽयं सनातनः।।	The soul cannot be divided, burnt, dissolved, or dried up. It is eternal, all-pervading, unalterable, unmoving, and without a beginning. 2/24
अव्यक्तोऽयमचिन्त्योऽयमविकार्योऽयमुच्यते। तस्मादेवं विदित्वैनं नानुशोचितुमर्हसि।।	It is said that the self cannot be seen, understood, or changed. Knowing this you should

	not mourn for the body. 2/25
अथ चैनं नित्यजातं नित्यं वा मन्यसे मृतम्। तथापि त्वं महाबाहो नैवं शोचितुमर्हसि।।	Even if you believe that the soul is continually born and dies continually, you still do not have any reason to lament for it. 2/26
जातस्य हि ध्रुवो मृत्युर्ध्रुवं जन्म मृतस्य च। तस्मादपरिहार्येऽर्थे न त्वं शोचितुमर्हसि।।	Birth and death are unavoidable matters. Do not lament over them because those who are born will certainly die one day and those who die will be born again one day. 2/27
त्वमादिदेवः पुरुषः पुराण स्वमस्य विश्वस्य परं निधानम्। वेत्तासि वेद्यं च परं च धाम त्वया ततं विश्वमनन्तरूप।।	You are the original Personality of Godhead, the oldest, the ultimate sanctuary of the entire universe. You are the knower and the knowledge. The supreme abode. The entire universe is pervaded by you. 11/38

REFERENCES

1. FAO. 2020. Global Forest Resources Assessment 2020 – Key findings. Rome. https://doi.org/10.4060/ca8753en

2. The data used in this chart comes from several sources.

Forests – this data is primarily sourced from the UN Food and Agriculture Organization (FAO). It provides long-term estimates on forest cover in 10,000 and 5,000 years BP. Its State of the World's Forests report provides estimates of global forest cover today, and rates of change over previous decades. In a related post we have combined this FAO data with global deforestation rates from Williams (2003) to document forest change over the last 300 years – this gives us data on forest change from 1700 onwards.

The definition of 'forest' can vary depending on aspects such as tree density and height. Absolute estimates of forest cover from other sources may differ for this reason. However, most align on the relative change in forests over this period. For example, Ellis et al. (2020). estimate a 35% loss of global forest cover since 10,000. This is very close to our estimate of a one-third loss.

Agricultural and urban land – The UN FAO Statistical database provides data on global agricultural and urban land from 1961 onwards. Pre-1961 land use is sourced from the work of Ellis et al. (2020).

FAO and UNEP. 2020. The State of the World's Forests 2020. Forests, biodiversity, and people. Rome.

Williams, M. (2003). Deforesting the earth: from prehistory to global crisis. University of Chicago Press.

3. The first series of data comes from Williams (2006), who estimates deforestation rates from 1700 to 1995.7 Due to poor data resolution, these are often given as average rates over longer periods – for example, annual average rates are given over the period from 1700 to 1849, and 1920 to 1949. That's why these rates look strangely consistent over a long time.

4. The second series comes from the UN Food and Agriculture Organization (FAO). It produces a new assessment of global forests every 5 years.8

5. FAO (2020). Global Forest Resources Assessment 2020: Main report. Rome. https://doi.org/10.4060/ca9825en.

6. The total forest cover in India (2023) is 7,13,789 square kilometers which is 21.71% of the total geographical area of the country. India added 1,540 sq km of forest cover from 2019 to 2021. The forest cover is divided into 3 parts.3 Apr 2023

7. Author: Garrison Frost, joined Save the Redwoods League in 2019 as its Director of Communications.

8. The Bhagavad Gita

9. God save the greens, Craig Brodersen, Times Evoke; TOI, Chennai June 24,2023

DISCLAIMER

This book is intended solely for informational purposes, aiming to shed light on the vital role the Kingdom of plants plays in sustaining life. The information presented herein, from the microscopic mosses to the towering trees, is offered as a means to enhance awareness and appreciation for the fundamental services plants provide—accounting for 80% of our daily sustenance and 98% of the oxygen we breathe.

The narratives within delve into the Plant kingdom's role as a repository for the Basic Life Supporting System (BLISS!), encompassing food, air, water, fertile soil, life-saving drugs, and the silent wisdom communicated akin to monks. The inclusion of the inspiring story of Hugo Wood, an IFS Officer in India, serves to inspire action towards the protection, conservation, and nurturing of our forests—the very roots of our survival.

This book is not a substitute for professional advice, and the author assumes no responsibility for any consequences resulting from the information presented. Readers are encouraged to seek professional guidance for specific situations and to act responsibly in their interactions with the botanical world. Your engagement with this book signifies your understanding of its informational nature and the importance of fostering a deeper connection with the plant kingdom.

ABOUT THE AUTHORS

 Both **Dr. Manoj Sarkar** and **Dr. Aruna Basu** are from the Indian Forest Service (retd.) and did their doctorate in Botany. They put in about 30 years of service as senior-level officers. Their cadre was allotted to Tamil Nadu.

They love Forests and plants. Both of them are prolific writers on plants in scientific journals and also in daily newspapers. Their books on botany, medicinal plants are published by the Tamil Nadu Govt and also by the Govt of India. The present book is part of a series on the author-niche 'Self-Mastery through the Kingdom of Plants' to create awareness, love, and care to protect the plant community and protect ourselves.

MAY WE ASK YOU A FAVOR?

At the outset, we want to give you a big thanks for reading this book. You could have chosen any other book, but you took ours, and we appreciate this. We hope you have at least a few actionable insights that will positively impact your daily life.

Can we ask for 30 seconds more of your time?

We'd love it if you could leave a review of the book. That will help us grow our readership by encouraging folks to take a chance on our books.

Keeping it straight - *reviews are the lifeblood of any author.*

It will take less than a minute of your time but will tremendously help us reach out to more people. **Kindly provide your review at the store you bought this book from.** And we'd love to see your review. Thanks for your support.

www.ingramcontent.com/pod-product-compliance
Lightning Source LLC
Chambersburg PA
CBHW051105250726
48656CB00001B/492